This Journal belongs to

___

51934741R10068

Made in the USA
Lexington, KY
07 September 2019